# shake, rattle, and roll

Exploring the Science of Earthquakes

## sarah michaels

# **contents**

# introduction

## welcome

Have you ever felt the ground shake beneath your feet, or heard about earthquakes happening in distant parts of the world? If you have, you might be curious about what causes these incredible natural events. And if you haven't, well, you're in for an adventure as we explore the secrets beneath the Earth's surface!

Earthquakes are one of nature's most powerful and intriguing phenomena. They can be small tremors that barely rattle a teacup, or massive quakes that can change landscapes forever. But what exactly is an earthquake? Simply put, an earthquake is what happens when the ground shakes due to energy being released from deep within the Earth. This energy release can be so strong that it's felt over vast areas, and it can happen suddenly, without any warning.

You might wonder where all this energy comes from. Our planet is like a giant puzzle made up of huge pieces called tectonic plates. These plates are always moving, but very, very slowly. Sometimes, they bump into each other, pull apart, or slide past one another. When this happens, energy builds up along the edges of the plates. Eventually, this energy needs to go somewhere, and that's when an earthquake happens!

Now, you might be thinking, "How can we study something that happens deep inside the Earth?" That's where scientists called seismologists come in. Seismologists are like detectives who study the Earth's movements. They use special tools called seismographs to record and measure earthquakes. By studying these records, they learn more about how and why earthquakes happen.

You see, every earthquake is unique. Some are so small that only sensitive instruments can detect them. Others are big enough to be felt by people and can even cause damage to buildings and roads. Earthquakes can occur anywhere in the world, but they're most common along the edges of those tectonic plates we talked about.

Understanding earthquakes is not only about science; it's also about safety. Knowing what to do during an earthquake can keep you and your family safe. For example, if you're indoors during an earthquake, you should drop to the ground, take cover under a sturdy table or desk, and hold on until the shaking stops. If you're outdoors, stay away from buildings, trees, and streetlights. These simple steps can make a big difference in staying safe during an earthquake.

But earthquakes aren't just about shaking ground. They can cause other natural events, like tsunamis, which are giant waves caused by earthquakes under the ocean. They can also trigger landslides in hilly or mountainous areas. Understanding these connections helps us prepare for and respond to these natural disasters better.

Did you know that people have been recording earthquakes for thousands of years? Ancient civilizations had their own ways of explaining and dealing with earthquakes. Today, we use science to understand them, but it's fascinating to learn about the myths and legends that cultures around the world have created about earthquakes.

As we explore the world of earthquakes together, you'll discover so much more than just facts and figures. You'll learn about the power and beauty of our planet, the importance of being prepared, and the exciting world of scientific discovery. Earthquakes are a reminder of how dynamic and ever-changing our planet is, and by learning about them, you become part of a community of young explorers who are curious about the world around them.

Remember, every question you ask and every discovery you make takes you one step closer to understanding the amazing planet we call home. And who knows? Maybe one day, you'll be the one helping to unlock more of Earth's mysteries!

## overview of earthquakes

Imagine you're standing on a rug and suddenly someone pulls it from under you. Whoa! You might stumble a bit, right? Earthquakes are a bit like that, but instead of a rug, it's the ground itself that shakes.

Earthquakes are natural events where the Earth's surface shakes and trembles. This shaking can be gentle and hardly noticeable, or it can be so strong that it can knock down entire buildings and cause huge cracks in the ground. But what causes the ground to shake like this?

Our planet is made up of several large pieces called tectonic plates. You can think of these plates like giant rafts floating on a slowly moving sea of molten rock, deep inside the Earth. These plates are always moving, but very, very slowly. Sometimes, they bump into each other, move apart, or grind past one another. This movement is usually so slow that you don't feel it. But sometimes, these plates get stuck at their edges due to friction. When the stress on the edge overcomes the friction, there is an earthquake that releases energy in waves that travel through the Earth's crust and cause the shaking that we feel.

Imagine holding a pencil between your fingers and bending it until it snaps. The sudden break releases energy, and the pencil makes a snapping sound. In an earthquake, the Earth's crust breaks like the pencil, but it releases much more energy. This energy travels through the Earth in waves, just like ripples on a pond after you throw a stone in it.

Now, you might be wondering, "How do we measure earthquakes?" Scientists use something called the Richter Scale to measure the strength of an earthquake. This scale starts at 0 and has no upper limit, but most earthquakes fall between 2 and 8. A higher number means a stronger earthquake. A quake of 2 or 3 is usually so small that you might not even feel it. But an earthquake of 6 or higher can cause serious damage.

One of the most astonishing things about earthquakes is how they show the dynamic nature of our planet. The Earth is not a static, unchanging place. It's always moving and transforming, even though we may not see it happening most of the time. Earthquakes remind us that our planet is alive with activity.

You might also wonder, "Do earthquakes happen everywhere?" While earthquakes can happen anywhere, they are more likely to occur near the edges of those tectonic plates. Places like California, Japan, and New Zealand are more prone to earthquakes because they're located on the edges of these plates.

Apart from the shaking, earthquakes can cause a lot of other things to happen. They can trigger landslides, where large amounts of earth and rock slide down a mountain or a hill. They can also cause tsunamis, which are huge ocean waves. When an earthquake happens under the sea, it can push up large volumes of water, creating a tsunami that can travel across entire oceans.

Now, let's talk a bit about the history of earthquakes. People have felt earthquakes for thousands of years, and they've always tried to understand them. In ancient times, people often thought earthquakes were caused by giant animals moving under the ground or by angry gods. Today, thanks to science, we know what really causes them.

Understanding earthquakes is not just about science; it's also about being prepared. Knowing what to do during an earthquake can help keep you safe. For example, it's important to stay calm and quickly find a safe place, like under a sturdy table or desk, and hold on until the shaking stops.

Throughout history, earthquakes have inspired many stories, myths, and legends. These stories show us how people from different cultures and times have tried to make sense of this powerful natural phenomenon. Today, we use scientific methods to study earthquakes, but these stories are still part of our rich cultural heritage.

As we continue to learn about earthquakes, we also learn more about our planet. Each earthquake is a clue that helps scientists understand the Earth's interior and its movements. By studying earthquakes, we can learn how to build safer buildings, predict when earthquakes might happen, and prepare better for when they do occur.

Remember, every time the ground shakes, it's an opportunity to learn something new about our planet. Earthquakes are a natural part of the Earth's cycle, and they play a big role in shaping the world we live in.

# 1 /
# understanding earthquakes

## how earthquakes occur

LET'S embark on an exciting journey to understand how these natural wonders occur. It's a bit like being a detective, piecing together clues to solve a mystery!

First off, let's talk about the Earth. Our planet isn't just a solid ball; it's more like an onion, made up of different layers. The outermost layer, where we live, is called the crust. Beneath the crust is the mantle, and deep inside the Earth is the core. But it's the crust where all the earthquake action happens.

The Earth's crust isn't one solid piece. It's broken up into big slabs called tectonic plates. Imagine a cracked eggshell, with each crack representing a boundary between the plates. These plates are floating on the mantle, which is made of super-hot, semi-solid rock. It's like how ice floats on water, except the 'ice' here are the tectonic plates, and the 'water' is the mantle.

These tectonic plates are always moving, but they move very, very slowly. We're talking about the speed at which your fingernails grow! Sometimes, these plates move away from each other, sometimes they move towards each other, and sometimes they slide past each other. Most of the time, this movement is so slow and steady that we don't feel a thing.

But here's where it gets interesting. The edges of these plates aren't smooth; they're rough and jagged. When they rub against each other, they can get stuck because of the friction. But even when they're stuck, the plates keep trying to move, and this builds up a lot of pressure. Think of it like stretching a rubber band. The more you stretch it, the more tension builds up.

Then, suddenly, when the pressure becomes too much, the plates suddenly snap and move. This sudden release of energy is what causes an earthquake. The point inside the Earth where this break happens is called the focus, and right above it on the surface is the epicenter. The energy released travels out from the focus in waves, shaking the ground as it moves – and that's what we feel during an earthquake.

These waves are a bit like the ripples you see when you drop a stone in a pond. There are different kinds of waves that travel in different ways. Some move up and down, some move side to side, and others roll along. These waves can travel long distances, and it's the energy in these waves that we feel during an earthquake.

It's also important to know that not all earthquakes are the same. Some are small and you might not even notice them. Others can be so big that they cause buildings to fall and roads to crack. The size of an earthquake depends on how much energy is released.

Scientists use special tools to measure earthquakes. One of the most common tools is called a seismograph. A seismograph records the waves caused by an earthquake. By studying these records, scientists can learn a lot about the earthquake, like where it happened, how deep it was, and how strong it was.

But why do we need to know about earthquakes? Understanding earthquakes helps us prepare for them. By knowing where earthquakes are likely to happen and how strong they might be, we can build safer buildings and homes. We can also teach people what to do during an earthquake to stay safe.

Earthquakes are a natural part of our planet's life. They've been happening for millions of years and will continue to happen. They're one way the Earth releases energy and keeps itself balanced. Even though they can be scary, they're also fascinating to learn about.

## tectonic plates and fault lines

Imagine you're piecing together a giant jigsaw puzzle of the Earth. That's exactly what we're about to do!

First off, let's talk about tectonic plates. Remember how we said the Earth's crust is like a cracked eggshell? These cracks divide the crust into big pieces called tectonic plates. These plates are huge! Some are as big as continents, while others are smaller. But what's truly fascinating is that these plates are always moving.

You see, the Earth is a bit like a slow cooker. Beneath the crust, in the mantle, there's a lot of heat. This heat causes the rock in the mantle to move in a slow, flowing pattern. Think of it like the goo in a lava lamp. This movement in the mantle is what causes the tectonic plates on the crust to shift and slide.

Now, where these tectonic plates meet is what we call fault lines. A fault line is like a crack on the surface of the Earth where two plates meet. There are different types of fault lines depending on how the plates move against each other. Some plates move apart, some move towards each other, and some slide past one another. Each type of movement creates different features on the Earth's surface and can cause different kinds of earthquakes.

When two plates move apart, it's called a divergent boundary. Imagine pulling a piece of stretchy cheese apart – that's what happens at these boundaries. As the plates move apart, magma from deep within the Earth rises up and forms new crust. This is how new ocean floors are created!

Then we have convergent boundaries, where two plates move towards each other. This can happen in a couple of ways. If an oceanic plate meets a continental plate, the denser oceanic plate gets pushed under the continental plate in a process called subduction. This can create deep ocean trenches and volcanic mountains. When two continental plates collide, they push against each other and form mountain ranges – like how the Himalayas were formed!

And finally, there are transform boundaries, where plates slide past each other. The most famous example of this is the San Andreas Fault in California. Here, the plates grind against each other, and this grinding can cause earthquakes.

Fault lines are like the Earth's weak spots. When the plates move, these are the places where the Earth's crust is most likely to crack and cause an earthquake. The energy that's released during an earthquake travels in waves from the focus, which is the starting point of the earthquake deep within the Earth, to the epicenter, which is the point right above the focus on the Earth's surface.

Understanding tectonic plates and fault lines is crucial in the study of earthquakes. By studying the movement of these plates, scientists can predict where earthquakes are more likely to occur. This helps in making buildings that are safer and preparing cities and towns for possible earthquakes.

But it's not just about safety. The movement of tectonic plates has shaped our planet over millions of years. It's the reason we have mountains and oceans. It's also the reason why continents look like pieces of a puzzle that fit together. Long ago, all the continents were joined together in a supercontinent called Pangaea. Over time, the tectonic plates moved and shifted to form the continents as we know them today.

Isn't it amazing to think about how our planet is always changing? Every mountain, every ocean, and every continent tells the story of the Earth's incredible journey through time.

# 2 /
# the science behind earthquakes

## how earthquakes are measured

HAVE you ever wondered how scientists figure out how strong an earthquake is? It's like a detective solving a mystery, but instead of looking for clues at a crime scene, they're measuring the shaking of the Earth.

First things first, let's talk about the Richter scale. Developed in the 1930s by Charles F. Richter, this scale measures the magnitude, or size, of an earthquake. Think of it like a ruler that measures how much the ground shakes during an earthquake. But instead of measuring in inches or centimeters, the Richter scale measures in 'magnitudes'.

The Richter scale starts at 0, which is hardly

noticeable, and can go beyond 9, which represents an incredibly powerful earthquake. The scale is logarithmic, which might sound super technical, but it's pretty simple when you break it down. A logarithmic scale means that each whole number increase on the Richter scale is actually ten times more powerful than the previous number. So, a magnitude 4 earthquake isn't just one step up from a magnitude 3 earthquake; it's actually ten times stronger!

Now, imagine a seismograph – a tool that scientists use to measure earthquakes. It's like a pen attached to a weight, suspended from a frame. When the Earth shakes, the frame moves, but the weight stays still, causing the pen to draw squiggly lines on a rolling piece of paper. These squiggly lines, called seismograms, show us how much the ground is moving.

Reading a seismogram can be fascinating. The bigger the squiggles, the bigger the earthquake. Scientists analyze these squiggles to figure out not only the magnitude of the earthquake but also where it started – the epicenter. It's like putting together the pieces of a puzzle to see the whole picture of an earthquake.

But here's something really interesting: the Richter scale isn't the only way to measure earthquakes. While it's great for measuring the energy released by small to medium earthquakes, it doesn't do as well with really large ones. That's where the Moment Magnitude Scale comes in. This scale, developed in the 1970s, is a bit more accurate for larger earthquakes. It measures the total energy released by an earthquake, and it's the scale that most scientists use today.

Measuring an earthquake's magnitude is crucial. It helps us understand how much energy was released and how much damage the earthquake might cause. But there's more to earthquakes than just how strong they are. Scientists also study the intensity of an earthquake – how much damage it causes and how people feel it.

The intensity of an earthquake can vary depending on where you are. If you're right at the epicenter, it's going to feel a lot stronger than if you're far away. And the type of ground you're on can make a difference too. Earthquakes tend to feel stronger on soft ground, like mud or sand, than on hard rock.

Now, let's talk about something really cool – predicting earthquakes. Scientists are always trying to find ways to predict when and where an earthquake will happen. While we're not quite there yet, we're getting better at understanding the signs that an earthquake might be coming. It's like being weather forecasters, but for the ground!

Earthquake measurement and prediction are important because they help us stay safe. By understanding where earthquakes are likely to happen and how strong they might be, we can build safer buildings, create better emergency plans, and teach people what to do during an earthquake.

# epicenter and aftershocks

Next, we're going to unravel some cool terms that are key to understanding earthquakes – 'epicenter' and 'aftershocks'. These words might sound a bit like something out of a superhero comic, but they're actually really important in the science of earthquakes.

Let's start with 'epicenter'. Imagine you're at a concert, right in front of the stage. The music is loudest where you are, isn't it? Now, think of an earthquake. If you could magically see underground where the earthquake starts, that point deep in the Earth is called the 'focus'. But directly above it, on the Earth's surface, is the epicenter. This is the spot right above where the earthquake begins, and it's usually where the strongest shaking is felt. It's like the center of a ripple in a pond when you throw in a stone – the point where everything starts.

Now, onto 'aftershocks'. Let's say you've just jumped off a diving board into a pool. After your big splash, there are smaller ripples that follow, right? Aftershocks are like those smaller ripples, but for earthquakes. After the main earthquake (which scientists call the 'mainshock'), there are usually smaller tremors that follow. These are after-shocks, and they can happen minutes, hours, days, or even months after the main earthquake!

Aftershocks can be pretty tricky. Sometimes they're so small that you hardly notice them, but other times they can be strong enough to cause more damage, especially if buildings or roads have already been weakened by the mainshock. Scien-tists keep a close eye on aftershocks because studying them helps to understand more about the main earthquake and the area's seismic activity.

Here's something interesting: not all aftershocks are weaker than the mainshock. Sometimes, an earthquake that was initially considered the main-shock is reclassified as a foreshock if a later earth-quake in the same area is larger. This switcheroo can be a bit surprising, just like when a movie has a plot twist you didn't see coming!

Understanding epicenters and aftershocks is

super important for several reasons. For one, it helps emergency services know where to send help first after an earthquake. They rush to the epicenter area because that's likely where the most help is needed. Also, by studying aftershocks, scientists can learn a lot about how the Earth's crust behaves after a big shake. This information can be crucial in making buildings and structures that are better able to withstand earthquakes.

But how do scientists figure out where the epicenter of an earthquake is? Well, they use data from seismographs all over the world. By looking at the time it takes for the seismic waves to reach each seismograph, they can calculate the distance of each seismograph from the epicenter. Then, by using a method called 'triangulation', which involves drawing circles on a map, they pinpoint the exact location of the epicenter. It's like solving a giant puzzle that spans the globe!

Now, let's talk about the impact of earthquakes and aftershocks. When an earthquake hits, it can change landscapes, form new faults, and even shift the position of the Earth's tectonic plates. After-shocks continue this process, sometimes changing the landscape even more. It's a bit like how a sculptor chisels away at a piece of marble, gradually changing its shape.

It's not just the physical landscape that's affected by earthquakes and aftershocks. People's lives can be greatly impacted too. That's why understanding these terms and the science behind them is so important. It helps us prepare for earthquakes and protect ourselves and our communities.

# experiments

Experiment 1: Make Your Own Mini Earthquake

For this experiment, you'll need a large tray, some sand, a few small houses made from blocks or cards, and a rubber ball.

1. Spread the sand evenly in the tray to represent the Earth's surface.

2. Place your little houses on the sand.

3. Now, gently tap the tray's side with the rubber ball to simulate an earthquake.

4. Observe how the houses react. Do they fall over with gentle taps or only with stronger ones?

This simple experiment shows how earthquakes affect structures differently depending on their strength. You can even try building houses of different shapes and sizes to see which ones withstand the 'earthquake' best.

Experiment 2: Understanding Seismic Waves

You'll need a large bowl of water and a small stone for this one.

1. Fill the bowl with water.

2. Drop the stone in the middle and watch the ripples that form.

3. The ripples are like seismic waves radiating out from the earthquake's epicenter.

Notice how the waves spread outwards in all directions and how they get smaller as they move away from the center. This is similar to how seismic waves from an earthquake diminish in strength as they travel away from the epicenter.

Experiment 3: Fault Line in Action

For this, you'll need a foam tray, some paint, a paintbrush, and a pair of scissors.

1. Cut the foam tray in half to create two separate pieces.

2. Paint a straight line across both pieces where they meet.

3. Once the paint dries, slowly slide one piece past the other and watch the line break and shift.

This experiment shows how fault lines work. When tectonic plates (represented by the foam pieces) move past each other, they can cause the Earth's crust (the line you painted) to break and shift, leading to earthquakes.

Experiment 4: Building an Earthquake-Proof Structure

Gather some marshmallows, toothpicks, and small weights (like coins or washers).

1. Use the marshmallows and toothpicks to build a small structure – it can be a tower, a bridge, or any design you like.

2. Once your structure is ready, gently place weights on it until it starts to wobble or collapse.

3. Try redesigning your structure to see if you can make it hold more weight.

This experiment helps you understand what makes buildings and structures more resistant to earthquakes. Architects and engineers use similar principles to design buildings that can withstand the shaking and trembling of an earthquake.

Experiment 5: Simulating Aftershocks

You'll need a tray of Jell-O and some small pebbles.

1. Make a tray of Jell-O and let it set. The Jell-O represents the Earth's crust.

2. Drop a pebble into the Jell-O to simulate the mainshock of an earthquake.

3. Then, gently drop more pebbles to represent aftershocks.

Observe how the Jell-O shakes and wobbles with each pebble drop. This shows how aftershocks can continue to affect an area even after the main earthquake has occurred.

Discussion and Discovery

After each experiment, take some time to talk about what you observed. What did you notice about how different structures reacted to the 'earthquake' in the first experiment? How did the seismic waves in the water bowl change as they moved outwards? What happened to the line on the foam pieces when you moved them? How did redesigning your structure in the fourth experiment help it hold more weight? What did the Jell-O demonstrate about aftershocks?

These experiments are not only fun but also a great way to see the concepts of earthquakes in action. By trying different methods and observing the outcomes, you're doing exactly what scientists do: experimenting, observing, and learning.

# 3 /
# famous earthquakes in history

## significant earthquakes around the world

EARTHQUAKES HAVE BEEN a part of Earth's story for millions of years, and by learning about them, we can understand more about how our planet works and how people have responded to these natural events.

Let's start with one of the most famous earthquakes in history: the Great San Francisco Earthquake of 1906. This earthquake struck the coast of Northern California on April 18, 1906. It was a massive quake, with a magnitude estimated to be around 7.9. The shaking was so powerful that it destroyed much of San Francisco, causing fires that burned for days. Over 3,000 people lost their lives, and it became a pivotal moment in earthquake studies.

Now, let's travel across the Pacific Ocean to Japan, a country that is no stranger to earthquakes. In 2011, Japan experienced one of the most powerful earthquakes ever recorded. Known as the Great East Japan Earthquake, it had a magnitude of 9.0. Not only did this earthquake cause tremendous damage on land, but it also triggered a massive tsunami, with waves reaching heights of up to 40 meters. The tsunami caused widespread destruction along Japan's northeastern coast and even led to a serious nuclear accident at the Fukushima Daiichi Nuclear Power Plant.

Next on our list is the 2004 Indian Ocean earthquake and tsunami. This was one of the deadliest natural disasters in recorded history, with an estimated 230,000 to 280,000 people losing their lives in 14 countries. The earthquake had a magnitude of 9.1–9.3 and caused the entire planet to vibrate. It was so powerful that it triggered a series of devastating tsunamis, with waves as high as 30 meters, impacting countries around the Indian Ocean.

Let's take a moment to visit Chile, home to the strongest earthquake ever recorded. The 1960 Valdivia Earthquake in Chile had a staggering magnitude of 9.5. It caused widespread damage in

Chile and led to tsunamis that affected Hawaii, Japan, the Philippines, and the west coast of the United States. The earthquake was so powerful that it actually altered the Earth's rotation slightly.

Another significant earthquake occurred in China in 1556. Known as the Shaanxi earthquake, it is believed to be the deadliest earthquake in recorded history. With an estimated magnitude of approximately 8.0, it caused widespread devastation in the Shaanxi province and surrounding areas, resulting in the deaths of approximately 830,000 people.

Let's also talk about the 1994 Northridge earthquake in California. With a magnitude of 6.7, it might not have been the strongest earthquake ever, but it was one of the costliest in U.S. history. The quake caused widespread damage to freeways, buildings, and homes in the Los Angeles area. It was a wake-up call for many in the United States about the importance of earthquake preparedness and building construction designed to withstand seismic shaking.

In Italy, the 1908 Messina earthquake reminds us that Europe is also vulnerable to seismic activity. This earthquake, along with the resulting tsunami, struck the regions of Sicily and Calabria and is considered one of the most catastrophic natural disasters in European history. The magnitude of the earthquake was around 7.1, and it resulted in the deaths of over 100,000 people.

These historical earthquakes show us just how powerful and impactful the Earth's movements can be. They also teach us about the resilience and strength of people who have rebuilt their lives and communities after such devastating events.

Every earthquake has a story, not just about the geological forces at play, but also about the human experiences and lessons learned. From the ancient ruins in Greece and Turkey that show evidence of seismic activity thousands of years ago to modern cities designed to withstand the Earth's tremors, earthquakes have shaped human history in count-less ways.

# where earthquakes occurred

Imagine having a time machine and a magic map that lets us travel to different parts of the world at various points in history.

Our adventure begins with a large, colorful world map. This isn't just any map; it's a special kind of map called a 'seismic map'. It shows us where significant earthquakes have occurred throughout history. Each earthquake is marked with a dot. Bigger dots represent more powerful earthquakes. The map is like a storybook, each dot telling a tale of a moment when the Earth moved.

Let's zoom in on our first location: San Francisco, 1906. On our map, we see a big dot on the western coast of the United States. Next to it is a timeline with the date April 18, 1906. This was the date of the great San Francisco earthquake. The timeline shows us a picture of the city before and after the quake, helping us understand the impact of this massive event.

Now, let's hop across the Pacific Ocean to Japan in 2011. On March 11, a massive dot appears on our map, near the eastern coast of Japan. This marks the Great East Japan Earthquake. Alongside the map, our timeline tells the story of the earthquake and the resulting tsunami. It shows us how the events unfolded minute by minute, giving us a clearer picture of that day.

Next, our magical map takes us to the Indian Ocean in 2004. Here, a large dot near the coast of Sumatra marks the spot of the 2004 Indian Ocean earthquake and tsunami. The timeline here is a bit different. Instead of just minutes and hours, it spans days, showing the after-effects of the tsunami in different countries around the Indian Ocean.

We travel next to South America, to Chile in

1960. On our map, a giant dot near Valdivia marks the most powerful earthquake ever recorded. The timeline for this event is filled with details about the earthquake, the resulting tsunamis, and the changes in landforms that occurred.

Let's turn our map's dial back several centuries to Shaanxi, China, in 1556. A dot appears in the heart of China, marking the location of the deadliest earthquake in recorded history. The timeline for this earthquake is a bit different from the others, filled with historical accounts and drawings, as photography wasn't around back then.

Moving forward in time, we land in Northridge, California, in 1994. Here, our map shows a dot near Los Angeles. The timeline for the Northridge earthquake gives us a minute-by-minute account of the earthquake, the aftershocks, and the rescue efforts that followed.

Our last stop is in Messina, Italy, in 1908. A dot on the toe of Italy's boot marks one of Europe's most devastating earthquakes. The timeline here tells a story of destruction and then rebirth, as the city was rebuilt from the ruins.

As we journey through these maps and timelines, we're not just learning about earthquakes; we're learning about history, geography, and the resilience of people. Each dot on the map and each event on the timeline tells us a story of how people came together to rebuild and recover from these natural disasters.

These maps and timelines are tools that help us understand the world around us. They show us that earthquakes are not just random events; they're part of the Earth's natural processes. They also remind us of the importance of being prepared and learning from the past.

# impact and recovery efforts

Earthquakes, as we've learned, are powerful natural events that can change landscapes and lives in an instant. But it's what happens after the shaking stops that can truly inspire us.

Let's take a closer look at the Great San Francisco Earthquake of 1906. After the quake, much of San Francisco was in ruins. But what happened next? People came together in extraordinary ways. Neighbors helped neighbors, and volunteers came from far and wide. They set up temporary shelters, provided food and medical care, and began the long process of rebuilding the city. It took years, but the people of San Francisco showed incredible resilience and determination.

Now, let's travel to Japan in 2011. After the

Great East Japan Earthquake and the devastating tsunami, the world witnessed one of the most remarkable recovery efforts. Despite the enormity of the disaster, the Japanese people responded with incredible strength. They worked tirelessly to clean up the debris, rebuild homes, and restore communities. One of the most inspiring stories is how they repaired a damaged road in just six days! It showed the world Japan's commitment to getting back on its feet.

The 2004 Indian Ocean earthquake and tsunami was a disaster of a massive scale, affecting several countries. The recovery efforts required international cooperation. Countries around the world sent aid, including food, medical supplies, and volunteers. Organizations and governments worked together to rebuild homes, schools, and infrastructure. It was a powerful reminder of how the global community can come together in times of need.

In Chile, following the 1960 Valdivia Earthquake, the response was swift. Despite the challenges of the earthquake's magnitude, the Chilean government and people embarked on a massive reconstruction effort. They rebuilt homes, schools, and public buildings, often improving on the original structures to make them more earthquake-resistant.

The Shaanxi earthquake in 1556, in what is now China, had a different recovery story. In those days, there was less understanding of earthquakes and fewer resources for recovery. However, even then, people showed resilience. They rebuilt their homes and lives, passing down stories of survival and recovery through generations.

The 1994 Northridge earthquake in California is another example of effective recovery. Following the quake, there was a significant effort to repair and rebuild damaged infrastructure, including highways and bridges. It was also a turning point for earthquake preparedness in the United States. Building codes were improved, and more resources were put into earthquake research and early warning systems.

In Italy, after the 1908 Messina earthquake, the response was both immediate and long-term. Temporary shelters were set up for those who had lost their homes, and there was a large international relief effort. The rebuilding of Messina was an opportunity to redesign the city. New buildings were constructed with better materials and designs to withstand future earthquakes.

In each of these stories, we see a common

thread – the incredible human spirit. People facing the most challenging circumstances worked together, supported each other, and built back stronger. Recovery from an earthquake is not just about rebuilding buildings; it's about communities coming together, supporting each other, and looking forward with hope.

These recovery efforts also teach us important lessons. We learn about the power of community, the importance of being prepared, and the need for buildings and infrastructure that can withstand earthquakes. Scientists and engineers study these events to learn how to better predict earthquakes and improve building designs.

# 4 /
# earthquake safety tips

## what to do during an earthquake

EARTHQUAKES CAN BE SCARY, but knowing what to do can make all the difference. Let's dive into some practical advice that can help you stay safe if the ground starts shaking.

1. Drop, Cover, and Hold On

Imagine you're in a room and suddenly the ground starts to shake. What do you do? The best thing to remember is "Drop, Cover, and Hold On." First, drop to your hands and knees. This position prevents you from being knocked down. Next, cover your head and neck with your arms. If you can, get under a sturdy table or desk for better protection. Finally, hold on to whatever shelter you're under. This helps keep you in place during the shaking.

## 2. Stay Indoors Until the Shaking Stops

If you're indoors when an earthquake hits, stay there. Moving around can be dangerous because things might be falling or breaking. Wait until the shaking stops before you try to leave. Once it's safe, calmly and carefully exit the building, watching out for debris or damaged areas.

## 3. If You're Outdoors, Move to an Open Area

What if you're outside when the earthquake starts? Move to an open area away from buildings, trees, streetlights, and utility wires. These can fall and hurt you during an earthquake. Once you're in an open space, drop, cover, and hold on.

## 4. Avoid Elevators

Elevators might seem like a quick way to escape if you're in a tall building, but they're not safe during an earthquake. They can malfunction, or the power can go out, leaving you trapped. Always use the stairs to exit a building after an earthquake.

5. If You're in a Car, Stop Safely

Driving during an earthquake can be tricky. If you feel the shaking while you're in a car, safely pull over to the side of the road and stop. Avoid stopping under bridges, overpasses, and power lines. Stay in the car with your seatbelt fastened until the shaking stops.

6. Practice Earthquake Drills

Just like fire drills, earthquake drills can help you know what to do in case of an earthquake. Practice "Drop, Cover, and Hold On" at home, school, and other places you spend time. Knowing what to do can help you stay calm during an actual earthquake.

7. Prepare an Emergency Kit

It's a great idea to have an emergency kit ready. Your kit should have water, non-perishable food, a flashlight, batteries, a first-aid kit, and any other essentials you might need for at least three days. Keep your kit in a place that's easy to reach.

## 8. Know Your Home's Safe Spots

Every home is different, so it's good to know the safest spots in your house. These are usually under sturdy furniture like tables or desks. Stay away from windows, large mirrors, and heavy objects that could fall.

## 9. Learn Basic First Aid

Learning some basic first aid can be really helpful. Knowing how to treat cuts, bruises, or other minor injuries can be important after an earthquake, especially if medical help isn't immediately available.

## 10. Talk to Your Family About an Emergency Plan

It's a great idea to have a plan with your family. Talk about where to meet if you get separated and how to contact each other. Make sure everyone knows the plan and what to do during an earthquake.

. . .

Remember, earthquakes can happen without warning, but being prepared can make a big difference. Knowing what to do can help keep you and your loved ones safe.

As we wrap up this chapter, let's remember that while earthquakes are powerful, our knowledge and preparedness are even more powerful. By learning what to do during an earthquake, we take important steps to protect ourselves and those around us.

And that's our journey through practical advice on what to do during an earthquake. Keep these tips in mind, practice them, and share them with your friends and family. Stay curious, keep learning, and always be prepared for whatever adventures come your way! Let's continue to explore and learn together, armed with knowledge and a spirit of adventure. Keep exploring, young adventurers, and stay safe on your journey through the wonders of our planet!

# checklist for earthquake preparedness

1. Create Your Earthquake Safety Zone:

- Find safe spots in every room of your home. Look for places like under sturdy tables or desks.

- Practice "Drop, Cover, and Hold On" in each of these safe spots.

- Make sure nothing heavy can fall on you in your safe spot, like bookshelves or picture frames.

2. Emergency Contacts:

- Have a list of important phone numbers, like your family, friends, doctor, and local emergency services.

- Make sure everyone in your family knows where this list is.

- Practice memorizing a few important numbers in case you don't have the list with you during an earthquake.

3. Earthquake Emergency Kit:

- Pack a backpack with essential items like water, non-perishable food, a flashlight, extra batteries, a first-aid kit, blankets, and some clothes.

- Don't forget personal items like medications, glasses, or contact lenses.

- Check your kit every few months to replace any used or expired items.

4. Home Preparation:

- Secure heavy furniture and appliances to the walls to prevent them from falling over.

- Install safety latches on cabinets to keep items from falling out.

- Check for and repair any deep cracks in ceilings or foundations.

5. Practice Earthquake Drills:

- Have regular earthquake drills with your family. This helps everyone remember what to do when an earthquake happens.

- Time how quickly and safely everyone can get to their safe spots.

- Discuss what went well and what you can improve after each drill.

6. Learn How to Shut Off Utilities:

- Learn where your gas, electricity, and water

shut-off controls are.

- Teach responsible family members how to turn them off if there's a leak or electrical issue after an earthquake.


7. Plan a Family Meeting Spot:

- Decide on a safe place outside your home to meet after an earthquake.

- Make sure it's in an open area away from buildings, trees, and power lines.

- Practice going to your meeting spot after your earthquake drills.


8. Earthquake Insurance and Important Documents:

- Talk to your parents about earthquake insurance for your home.

- Keep copies of important documents like birth certificates and passports in a safe, accessible place.


9. Educate Yourself and Family:

- Read books and watch videos about earthquake safety.

- Attend a local earthquake preparedness workshop or training.

10. Help Others Prepare:

- Share what you've learned with friends and neighbors.

- Make a small emergency kit for your school backpack.

- Encourage friends to practice earthquake drills too.

Remember, being prepared for an earthquake is like being a superhero. You're not only keeping yourself safe, but you're also helping to protect those around you. Each step you take in preparing makes you more ready for the unexpected.

## safe and unsafe practices

1. The Safe Spots:

Our first illustration shows a family in their living room when an earthquake strikes. On the left side of the picture, we see the unsafe practice: standing in a doorway or running outside. On the right side, the family is doing the safe thing: they're each under sturdy pieces of furniture, like a strong table, covering their heads and necks with their arms. This picture is a powerful reminder of the "Drop, Cover, and Hold On" rule.

2. Preparing Your Home:

The next page has a fun, interactive illustration of a house. Parts of the house are clickable, revealing safe and unsafe practices. For example, clicking on a bookshelf shows it tipping over (unsafe) and then secured to the wall (safe). A water heater is first unstrapped (unsafe), then properly secured (safe). This interactive element makes learning about home safety both engaging and memorable.

3. What Not to Do:

Here we have a colorful comic strip showing common mistakes people make during an earthquake. One frame shows someone trying to run outside during the shaking, and in another, someone is standing in a doorway. Text bubbles explain why these actions are unsafe. This visual narrative helps us understand the risks of common misconceptions about earthquake safety.

. . .

4. Outdoor Safety:

This page features an illustration of a park with children playing. It splits into two scenarios: In one, kids are running towards trees and a building (unsafe), and in the other, they move to an open area away from potential hazards (safe). This illustration is a clear and simple guide on what to do if you're outside when an earthquake hits.

5. Post-Earthquake Safety:

On this page, we have a before-and-after illustration. The first part shows unsafe post-earthquake actions, like immediately running inside a building or using elevators. The second part depicts safe practices, like checking for hazards, using stairs, and gathering at the pre-decided family meeting spot. This visual comparison teaches us how to act once the shaking stops.

6. Car Safety:

This illustration shows two cars during an earthquake. In one scenario, the car is parked under an overpass (unsafe), and in the other, it's parked in an open area away from trees and build-ings (safe). This image is an excellent guide for what to do if you're in a car when an earthquake occurs.

## 7. Emergency Kit:

We have a bright and detailed illustration of an emergency kit, with each item clearly labeled. The safe practice here is having a fully stocked kit, while the unsafe practice is shown by a nearly empty kit. This picture makes the concept of preparing an emergency kit engaging and easy to understand.

## 8. Helping Others:

In this heartwarming illustration, we see people helping each other after an earthquake. One side shows unsafe actions, like ignoring someone calling for help, while the other side shows safe and kind actions, like providing first aid and comforting others. This illustration not only teaches safety but also the value of compassion and community.

# 5 /
# the role of
# scientists

## geologists and seismologists

### WHAT IS A GEOLOGIST?

A geologist is like a detective for the Earth. They study the Earth's surface and what it's made of. Imagine looking at a rock and being able to tell a story about how old it is or what the Earth was like when that rock was formed. That's what geologists do! They look at mountains, valleys, volcanoes, and even tiny grains of sand to learn about Earth's history.

One cool thing about geologists is that they often get to work outside. They might climb mountains, explore caves, or travel to the bottom of the ocean.

They collect samples like rocks, soil, and fossils and then analyze them to learn more about the Earth.

What is a Seismologist?

A seismologist is a type of geologist who specializes in studying earthquakes. They're like earthquake detectives! Seismologists use special tools called seismographs to record the shaking of the ground. These tools help them figure out where an earthquake happened, how strong it was, and what caused it.

Seismologists also try to understand how earthquakes affect the Earth and people. They study how buildings react to shaking and how to make them safer. They even work on predicting where and when the next earthquake might happen!

A Day in the Life of a Geologist and Seismologist

Let's imagine what a day in the life of a geologist or seismologist might be like. Our geologist starts the day by hiking up a mountain to collect rock samples.

She's studying how the mountain was formed. She takes notes, photographs the landscape, and uses a GPS device to record the location of her samples.

Meanwhile, our seismologist is in a lab, looking at data from seismographs around the world. He's analyzing the waves from a recent earthquake to learn more about it. He also checks maps and computer models to study the Earth's moving plates and identify areas that might be at risk for future earthquakes.

Why Their Work is Important

The work of geologists and seismologists is super important. They help us understand natural disasters like earthquakes and volcanoes. This knowledge can save lives by helping us prepare for these events. For example, if we know where earthquakes are likely to happen, we can build stronger buildings and homes in those areas.

Geologists also help us find important resources like water, minerals, and fossil fuels. They study the Earth to figure out where we can find these resources and how to get them safely.

Becoming a Geologist or Seismologist

Maybe you're thinking, "How can I become a geologist or seismologist?" Well, it starts with being curious about the Earth and loving science. Geologists and seismologists usually study Earth sciences or geology in college. They learn about rocks, minerals, fossils, and how the Earth's surface changes.

But learning about the Earth isn't just for geologists and seismologists. Anyone can be an Earth explorer! You can start by observing the rocks, soil, and landscapes around you. Maybe you'll collect rocks and learn about their different types. Or perhaps you'll watch a documentary about volcanoes or earthquakes. There's a whole world of Earth science waiting for you to discover!

# how they study earthquakes and predict them

The Tools of the Trade

First, let's talk about the tools that seismologists use. The most important one is the seismograph. It's a super-sensitive instrument that can detect even the tiniest shakes and rumbles of the Earth. When an earthquake happens, it records the vibrations in wiggly lines on a paper or a computer screen. These lines are called seismograms, and they look a bit like the squiggly lines you draw with a pen.

Seismologists study these seismograms to learn about earthquakes. They can tell how strong the earthquake was, how deep it was under the Earth's surface, and even how far away it was. It's like reading the Earth's own handwriting!

Detecting Earthquake Waves

Did you know that earthquakes send out different kinds of waves? Seismologists study these waves to learn more about earthquakes. There are two main types: P-waves and S-waves. P-waves are like the first rumbles of thunder - they come first and travel fast. S-waves are slower, but they move the ground back and forth. By studying the time it takes for these waves to reach different seismograph stations, seismologists can figure out where the earthquake happened. It's like a game of cosmic hide and seek!

## The Art of Prediction

Now, predicting earthquakes is really tough. Unlike weather forecasts, where we can see storm clouds brewing, earthquakes happen deep underground, and we can't see them coming. But seismologists are like weather forecasters for the Earth. They look for patterns and signs that might tell us where the next earthquake could happen.

One way they do this is by studying earthquake history. They look at where earthquakes have happened before and how often they occur in those places. It's like looking at old family photos to predict who you might look like when you grow up!

. . .

Seismologists also study the Earth's tectonic plates. These are huge slabs of rock that make up the Earth's surface, and they're always moving, really slowly. Most earthquakes happen along the edges of these plates. By monitoring how the plates move and where they rub against each other, seismologists can identify places where earthquakes are more likely to happen.

The Challenge of Prediction

Predicting exactly when an earthquake will happen is still beyond our reach. It's like trying to guess when a piece of popcorn will pop in the microwave. But seismologists are working on it. They use computers to create models of the Earth's movements and try to guess where the stresses are building up. These models are getting better all the time, but there's still a lot to learn.

How This Helps Us

Even though we can't predict earthquakes perfectly, studying them helps us in many ways. We can build safer buildings, especially in places where earthquakes are common. We can train people on what to do when an earthquake happens. And we can set up warning systems that give us a few seconds to take cover before the shaking starts.

Earthquake Scientists are Superheroes

Seismologists and geologists are like super-heroes of the Earth. They help us understand our planet and keep us safe from its rumbling powers. They show us that science is not just about knowing things but also about helping people.

# 6 /
# earthquake myths and facts

## common myths about earthquakes

MYTH 1: Earthquakes Can Be Predicted

Have you ever heard someone say they know when the next earthquake will happen? It sounds exciting, like knowing the future! But in reality, predicting the exact time and location of an earthquake is something even the smartest scientists can't do yet. While seismologists can identify areas that are likely to experience earthquakes, they can't say for certain when one will occur. It's like trying to guess when a hidden cookie jar will be opened - you know it's there, but you can't be sure when someone will open it.

. . .

## Myth 2: Big Earthquakes Always Cause Tsunamis

When we hear about underwater earthquakes, we often think of giant tsunamis, like in movies. However, not all underwater quakes cause tsunamis. For a tsunami to occur, the earthquake must be strong enough and happen in a way that displaces a large amount of water. Some underwater quakes are too weak or too deep to cause this. It's like splashing in a bathtub - small splashes don't overflow the tub, but big ones might!

## Myth 3: Animals Can Predict Earthquakes

Stories abound of animals acting strangely before an earthquake. While it's true that some animals might sense an earthquake a few seconds before humans, they can't predict them days or hours in advance. Animals are sensitive to the initial weak waves (P-waves) that humans can't feel. But as for predicting earthquakes long before they happen, our animal friends are just as surprised as we are.

## Myth 4: Standing in a Doorway is the Safest Place During an Earthquake

This one is a classic! In the past, when houses

were not as sturdily built, doorframes were sometimes the only thing left standing after an earthquake. But nowadays, with better building codes and construction, doorways aren't any stronger than the rest of the building. Plus, the swinging door can injure you. It's safer to "Drop, Cover, and Hold On" under a sturdy piece of furniture.

Myth 5: Small Earthquakes Prevent Big Ones

Some people think that small earthquakes relieve pressure between tectonic plates, preventing larger ones. However, the energy released in small earthquakes is not nearly enough to prevent larger ones. It's like thinking popping small bubbles in bubble wrap can stop the big bubbles from bursting.

Myth 6: Earthquakes Only Happen in the Morning

Imagine if earthquakes had a schedule, like a school bell! But earthquakes don't have a specific time when they are more likely to occur. They can happen any time of the day or night, throughout the year. Their timing is as random as when a leaf decides to fall from a tree.

. . .

Myth 7: All Earthquakes Cause the Ground to Open Up

The dramatic images of the ground splitting open during an earthquake are more a creation of movies and TV shows. In reality, while the ground does shake and can crack during an earthquake, it doesn't usually split open like a giant chasm. The movements of tectonic plates during an earthquake typically don't cause such dramatic openings.

Myth 8: California Will Eventually Fall into the Ocean

This is a big one! Some people believe that California will break off and fall into the sea because of earthquakes. But geologists assure us that this won't happen. The San Andreas Fault, which runs through California, is a place where two plates are sliding past each other, not apart. So, California isn't going anywhere - it's just on the move!

# factual information to debunk myths

Fact 1: Earthquake Prediction is Currently Impossible

While scientists have made leaps in understanding where earthquakes are more likely to occur, predicting the exact time and location of an earthquake is not possible with current technology. Earthquakes are complex geological processes influenced by many factors underground that we can't fully observe or measure yet. Scientists use probabilities based on historical data to estimate the likelihood of future earthquakes, but they cannot predict them precisely.

Fact 2: Not All Earthquakes Cause Tsunamis

Tsunamis are large, powerful waves caused by the displacement of a large volume of water, often due to underwater earthquakes. However, not all underwater earthquakes cause tsunamis. The movement of the Earth's crust during the quake needs to displace water significantly for a tsunami to occur. This usually happens with earthquakes that are strong (usually above magnitude 7.0), shallow, and occur near or under the ocean.

Fact 3: Animals and Earthquake Prediction

While there are anecdotal reports of animals behaving unusually before earthquakes, there's no scientific evidence that animals can predict earthquakes. Animals might sense the first, weak waves

(P-waves) of an earthquake before humans do, but these waves occur seconds to minutes before the stronger shaking is felt, not days or hours in advance.

## Fact 4: The Doorway Myth

The idea that standing in a doorway is the safest place during an earthquake is outdated. This belief originated from observing adobe houses, where door frames were sometimes the only structure left standing after an earthquake. In modern buildings, doorways are no safer, and the swinging of the door can cause injuries. The safest action during an earthquake is to drop, cover, and hold on under a sturdy piece of furniture.

## Fact 5: Small Earthquakes and Large Ones

Small earthquakes do not necessarily prevent larger ones. In fact, a series of small earthquakes can sometimes be foreshocks to a larger event. The energy released in small earthquakes is not enough to relieve the stress in the Earth's crust that leads to large earthquakes.

· · ·

Fact 6: Earthquakes Can Happen at Any Time

Earthquakes do not have a specific time of occurrence. They can happen at any time of the day or night, any day of the year. The timing of earthquakes is random and not influenced by human activities or the time of day.

Fact 7: Earth's Surface During Earthquakes

While the ground shakes and can crack during an earthquake, it rarely opens up in the dramatic fashion often depicted in movies. The type of ground movement that creates gaping chasms is extremely rare and not a typical feature of most earthquakes.

Fact 8: California and the San Andreas Fault

The San Andreas Fault is a transform fault, where two tectonic plates slide past each other. This movement does not lead to California "falling into the ocean." Instead, the motion is mostly horizontal, so while the landscape may change over millions of years, California won't drop off into the sea.

# 7 /
# activities and experiments

## diy projects related to earthquakes

**1**. Building a Simple Seismograph

A seismograph is an instrument that scientists use to record the vibrations of the Earth, like during an earthquake. We're going to make a simple version of this using everyday items.

What You Need:
- A shoebox
- A thick marker or a small paint roller
- Some string
- A small weight (like a fishing sinker or a small stone)
- Paper

- Scissors

Instructions:

1. Cut a small hole in one end of the shoebox.

2. Thread the string through the hole and tie the weight to one end so it hangs down inside the box.

3. Attach the marker or paint roller to the string, just above the weight. Make sure it can move freely.

4. Line the inside of the shoebox with paper.

5. When the Earth shakes, the weight will stay still while the box moves, causing the marker to draw lines on the paper. This is your seismic activity!

## 2. Earthquake-Proof Building Challenge

Let's put on our engineering hats and try to build a structure that can withstand an earthquake!

What You Need:

- Marshmallows

- Toothpicks

- Gelatin or a shallow pan filled with Jell-O (to simulate shaking ground)

- Small weights (like coins)

Instructions:

1. Use the marshmallows and toothpicks to build a structure. It can be a tower, a bridge, or any shape you like.

2. Once your structure is ready, place it on the gelatin or Jell-O.

3. Gently shake the pan to simulate an earthquake.

4. Add weights to your structure and see how much shaking it can take before it falls.

5. Modify your design to make it sturdier and try again!

3. Liquefaction in a Jar

Earthquake liquefaction happens when loose, wet soil starts acting like a liquid during an earthquake. We can simulate this with a simple experiment.

What You Need:

- A large clear jar with a lid
- Sand

- Water
- Small toy buildings or Lego structures

Instructions:

1. Fill the jar about halfway with sand and mix in enough water to make the sand wet but not submerged.

2. Place your toy buildings on top of the sand.

3. Seal the jar and shake it hard.

4. Watch as the buildings sink into the sand, just like buildings can sink into the ground during real-life liquefaction.

## 4. Create Your Own Earthquake Waves

Let's visualize how seismic waves move through the Earth with this fun project.

What You Need:

- A long, flexible coil or slinky
- Two chairs
- A helper

Instructions:

1. Stretch the coil or slinky between two chairs, with you and your helper holding each end.

2. One of you should quickly push and pull the end of the slinky to mimic P-waves, and then move it side to side for S-waves.

3. Observe how the waves travel along the slinky – this is similar to how seismic waves travel through the Earth.

5. Earthquake in a Pan

This project helps us understand how different structures react to earthquakes.

What You Need:

- A large baking pan or a shallow box
- Sand
- Different small objects to act as buildings (e.g., blocks, small boxes)
- A ball to simulate the earthquake

Instructions:

1. Fill the pan or box with sand and place your 'buildings' on top.

2. Tap the side of the pan with the ball to simulate earthquake vibrations.

3. Observe how different structures (tall, short, wide, narrow) react to the shaking. This helps us learn which shapes and sizes are more stable during an earthquake.

## quizzes and puzzles

Quiz Time!

Let's start with a quiz. For each question, choose the answer you think is correct. Ready? Here we go!

1. What is the main tool used by seismologists to measure earthquakes?

   a) Telescope

   b) Seismograph

   c) Barometer

   d) Compass

2. Which type of seismic wave arrives first at a seismograph station?

   a) S-wave

   b) P-wave

c) Love wave

d) Rayleigh wave

3. True or False: Small earthquakes can prevent larger ones from happening.

a) True

b) False

4. What do you do during an earthquake?

a) Run outside

b) Drop, Cover, and Hold On

c) Stand in a doorway

d) Jump up and down

5. Where do most earthquakes occur?

a) In the sky

b) Along tectonic plate boundaries

c) In the ocean only

d) On the moon

Answers:

1. b) Seismograph

2. b) P-wave

3. b) False

4. b) Drop, Cover, and Hold On

5. b) Along tectonic plate boundaries

## Earthquake-Themed Riddles

And now, for some fun riddles!

1. I shake the ground but am not an angry giant. I might be strong or weak, but I'm always important to scientists. What am I?

- Answer: An Earthquake

2. I travel fast and reach you first, but I'm not a sprinter in a race. I'm part of an earthquake. What am I?

- Answer: A P-wave

3. I'm a wave, but I don't live in the ocean. I move the ground in an earthquake. What am I?

- Answer: An S-wave

# conclusion

## key learning points

1. Earthquakes and Their Causes

We learned that earthquakes are caused by the movement of tectonic plates beneath the Earth's surface. These gigantic plates are always shifting, and when they rub against each other, they create energy that can lead to earthquakes. Imagine two giant puzzle pieces under the Earth that don't always fit perfectly. Sometimes they get stuck, and when they finally move, the Earth shakes!

2. Measuring Earthquakes

Remember the seismograph? This tool helps scientists, known as seismologists, measure earthquakes. They use it to record the vibrations in the

Earth, creating wiggly lines called seismograms. By studying these lines, seismologists can tell us how strong an earthquake was and where it happened. It's like a secret code hidden in the wiggles!

### 3. Types of Seismic Waves

We discovered that there are different types of waves that earthquakes produce. P-waves, which are the fastest, arrive first at a seismograph station. Then come the S-waves, which move the ground up and down or side to side. Understanding these waves helps scientists figure out the earthquake's epicenter – the point on the Earth's surface right above where the quake starts.

### 4. The Richter Scale

The Richter Scale, remember that? It's a way to measure the magnitude, or strength, of an earthquake. The scale starts at zero and goes up, with each number increase meaning the earthquake is ten times more powerful. A small earthquake might measure around 2 or 3, but a big, damaging one could be over 6!

### 5. Earthquake Safety

We also learned some vital tips on how to stay safe during an earthquake. The best thing to do is

"Drop, Cover, and Hold On." Find a sturdy table or desk, get under it, and protect your head and neck. And remember, don't run outside or stand in doorways – those are old ideas that we now know aren't safe.

## 6. Preparing for Earthquakes

Being prepared is key! We talked about making an earthquake emergency kit with water, food, a flashlight, and other essentials. It's also important to know your home's safe spots and have a plan with your family on where to meet after an earthquake.

## 7. Earthquake Myths

Our journey wouldn't be complete without busting some common earthquake myths. No, animals can't predict earthquakes, and small quakes don't prevent big ones. And California won't fall into the ocean because of the San Andreas Fault. These are just stories, and now you know the real science!

## 8. Fun with Earthquake Science

Remember when we made our own seismograph and tried to build an earthquake-proof structure? Those hands-on activities were not just fun, but they also helped us understand how earthquakes work and how we can study them.

9. The Role of Geologists and Seismologists

We met some amazing scientists who study earthquakes. Geologists look at rocks and the Earth's surface, while seismologists focus specifically on earthquakes. They're like detectives, unraveling the mysteries of the Earth.

# further exploration

The Never-Ending Adventure of Learning

Remember, learning is like a never-ending adventure, full of surprises and new paths to explore. Every question you ask opens a door to new knowledge. Think of each question as a stepping stone leading you to discover more about the Earth and its incredible phenomena.

Exploring Beyond the Book

Books are just the starting point. There's a whole world out there waiting for you to explore. Visit science museums or planetariums, where you can see models of the Earth's layers and even experience simulated earthquakes. Many museums also hold workshops and interactive sessions for young learners like you.

Joining Science Clubs

Check if your school or community has a science club. Being part of a club can be a lot of fun – you get to meet other kids who are just as curious as you are. You can work on science projects together, like building a better model of a seismograph or creating an earthquake preparedness campaign for your school.

Observing the World Around You

Be an observer. Next time you're outside, look at the landscape around you. Can you see any evidence of geological activity, like hills formed by ancient earthquakes? Even the patterns of cracks in the sidewalk can tell a story of movement and change.

Asking Experts

If you have questions, don't hesitate to ask a teacher or a local scientist. Many scientists love sharing their knowledge and might even show you some cool, hands-on experiments to help understand earthquakes better.

## Using Technology

The internet is a vast resource. Watch educational videos, participate in online science forums, or follow geology blogs. There are many apps and online simulations that can help you visualize how tectonic plates move and how earthquakes happen.

## Science Fairs and Projects

Participate in science fairs. They are great platforms to showcase what you've learned and to learn from others. You might consider creating a project that focuses on earthquake safety or the science behind seismic activity.

## Visiting Local Geological Sites

If you live near a geological site or a science center, take a trip with your family or school. Seeing geological formations in person is a fantastic way to understand the forces that shape our planet.

## Reading and Researching

There's always more to read and learn. Look for books and documentaries about earthquakes, volcanoes, and geology. They can provide deeper insights and answer questions you might have.

## Staying Informed

Keep up with the news about recent earthquakes around the world. It helps connect what you learn with real events. Understanding the impact of these earthquakes can also show you how important it is to learn and prepare.

The Power of Imagination

Never underestimate your imagination. It's a powerful tool that can take you on fantastic journeys. Imagine you're a scientist studying earthquakes, or a reporter covering an earthquake event. What would you do? How would you explain it to others?

Writing and Sharing

Share your knowledge with others. You could write articles, make a blog, or even start a YouTube channel about earthquakes and geology. Teaching others is a great way to deepen your own understanding.

The Future of Earthquake Science

And finally, think about the future. Science is always advancing. Maybe one day, you'll contribute to new ways of predicting earthquakes or inventing safer building technologies. The possibilities are endless.

# glossary

1. Earthquake

An earthquake is the shaking of the Earth's surface caused by the movement of the Earth's plates. Imagine the Earth's surface is like a cracked eggshell, and when these pieces move, we feel an earthquake.

2. Seismology

Seismology is the study of earthquakes and the waves they produce in the Earth. It's like being a detective, but instead of solving crimes, seismologists solve the mysteries of the Earth's movements.

3. Tectonic Plates

These are huge slabs of the Earth's crust that fit together like a jigsaw puzzle. The Earth's surface is made up of these plates, and their movement is what causes most earthquakes.

## 4. Seismograph

This is a tool that scientists use to record and measure the vibrations from earthquakes. Think of it as a super-sensitive pen that draws lines on paper whenever the Earth shakes.

## 5. Magnitude

Magnitude measures the size, or strength, of an earthquake. It tells us how much energy was released during the quake. The Richter scale, which we often hear about, is one way to measure magnitude.

## 6. Epicenter

The epicenter is the point on the Earth's surface directly above where an earthquake starts. If an earthquake were a splash in a pond, the epicenter would be right where the stone hit the water.

## 7. Fault

A fault is a crack in the Earth's crust where earthquakes often occur. It's like a weak spot where the Earth's plates can move, creating earthquakes.

8. P-Waves

These are primary waves that are the first to arrive at a location after an earthquake. They move quickly and travel through both solids and liquids. P-waves are like the first rumble of thunder you hear in a storm.

9. S-Waves

Secondary waves, or S-waves, arrive after P-waves. They move the ground up and down or side to side. S-waves can only travel through solids, not liquids.

10. Aftershock

Aftershocks are smaller earthquakes that happen after the main earthquake. They are like the smaller ripples that come after the initial big splash in a pond.

11. Richter Scale

This is a scale used to measure the strength, or magnitude, of an earthquake. Developed by Charles F. Richter, it helps us understand how powerful an earthquake was.

12. Seismic Waves

These are the waves of energy caused by an

earthquake. There are different types, including P-waves and S-waves, which travel through the Earth.

## 13. Liquefaction

This happens when the shaking of an earthquake turns solid ground into a liquid-like state. It's like when wet sand at the beach becomes squishy and watery when you step on it.

## 14. Subduction Zone

This is a place where one tectonic plate slides underneath another. Subduction zones are often sites of powerful earthquakes and volcanic activity.

## 15. Tsunami

A tsunami is a large, powerful wave caused by an underwater earthquake, a volcanic eruption, or a landslide. It's like a giant wall of water that can travel across oceans.

## 16. Geology

Geology is the study of the Earth, its materials, and the processes that shape it over time. If you love rocks, fossils, and learning about how mountains and valleys are formed, geology is for you!

17. Plate Tectonics

This is the theory that explains how the Earth's tectonic plates move and interact with each other. It's the big picture of how and why earthquakes, volcanoes, and mountain ranges happen.

# further reading and resources

Websites for Wiggly Learning

1. US Geological Survey (USGS) Earthquake Hazards Program [earthquake.usgs.gov]: This site is a goldmine of information. It has real-time earthquake data, educational resources, and lots of interesting earthquake facts.

2. National Geographic Kids [kids.nationalgeographic.com]: Search for earthquakes on this site to find fun facts, amazing photos, and interesting articles tailored for young minds.

3. Fun Science Demos [youtube.com/funsciencedemos]: This YouTube channel has some cool videos on earthquakes, explaining complex concepts in fun, easy-to-understand ways.

4. Science Kids [sciencekids.co.nz]: Head to the 'Earth Science' section for fun earthquake facts and experiments you can try at home.

Museums That Rock

1. The Natural History Museum, London: Their Earthquake exhibit lets you experience the power of a quake and learn about the science behind it.

2. The American Museum of Natural History, New York: Visit their Earth and Planetary Sciences halls to learn about the forces that shape our planet, including earthquakes.

3. The Pacific Science Center, Seattle: Check out their awesome Planet Earth exhibit, where you can learn about earthquakes and even create your own.

4. The California Academy of Sciences, San Francisco: Their exhibits on earthquakes are not only informative but also interactive, making learning a fun experience.

Apps to Shake Things Up

1. MyShake: Developed by UC Berkeley, this app uses your phone's sensors to detect earthquake shaking and gathers data for seismologists.

2. QuakeFeed Earthquake Map, Alerts, and News: This app provides real-time earthquake alerts and information, making it a handy tool for keeping updated.

50300857R00059